OXFORD POETS 2004

The editors of this anthology are members of the Oxford*Poets* Board.

David Constantine is an authority on Hölderlin, as well as a poet and translator. His most recent collection is *Something for the Ghosts* (Bloodaxe, 2002).

Bernard O'Donoghue teaches medieval English at Wadham College, Oxford and has published five books of poems, of which the most recent is *Outliving* (Chatto, 2003).

Also available from Carcanet/Oxford*Poets*

Oxford Poets 2000
Oxford Poets 2001
Oxford Poets 2002

Oxford*Poets* 2004

an anthology edited by
David Constantine and
Bernard O'Donoghue

Oxford*Poets*
CARCANET

First published in Great Britain in 2004 by Carcanet Press Limited
Alliance House
Cross Street
Manchester M2 7AQ

A CIP catalogue record for this book is available from the British Library

ISBN 1 903039 66 5

The publisher acknowledges financial assistance
from Arts Council England

Set in Palatino by XL Publishing Services, Tiverton
Printed and bound in England by SRP Ltd, Exeter

Contents

Julian Stannard

Greg Sweetnam

Introduction

This is our fourth anthology. As in our previous anthologies, the poets here are various and distinctive. Some may be known already, from publication elsewhere; others will be new to most readers. They vary in provenance, concerns, tones of voice, and lyric strategies, but have in common the qualities we are on the lookout for: seriousness of purpose, honesty and liveliness. They pay attention to the real world.

Several of the poets so far presented in our anthologies have written even better and have been published more widely since. Their success encourages us. We wish this series to be distinctive – its qualities recognisable – but also to be alert and open-minded to good new poems wherever they may come from, in whatever shape.

KAREN ANNESEN

Karen Annesen was born in Florida in 1964 and grew up on Cape Cod, Massachusetts. After completing a first degree in psychology she moved to the UK where she has lived, worked and studied for the past fourteen years. She was recently awarded an M.Phil in Writing from the University of Glamorgan and combines working in the field of homelessness and domestic violence with being a part-time creative writing tutor for the WEA and the City Lit. She won a Hawthornden Fellowship in 1997.

Some of the poems in this anthology have appeared previously in *PN Review*, *The Yellow Crane*, *The Magazine* and *Oxford Magazine*.

Unsteady

She left her Bible behind
the night it rained and rained
and rained. They were somewhere
between Georgia and Alabama
when the car started to stutter

and shake then finally die.
He was getting grease on his jacket,
well it was his brother's really
and she who had felt like an angel
in her second-hand wedding gown

suddenly saw in the rear-view mirror
all that was and would be
and she wanted to speak then
and not hold her peace,
but the engine was roaring again
and he was signing to her,
thumbs up, *all is well*.

Bridesmaid

Her veil blows across my face,
my hand tight in hers on the way to the church.
We might be skipping along, seven and eight
except for that veil. The lace scratches
and I wonder again about her choice.
Why white at twenty-eight?
Mr Miller cuts the lawn – twice a week still.
His wife weeds the borders
humming a tune I can't make out.
I'm in apricot, last time pink.
My hand is sweating, or is it hers?
The church will be cool,
Father Peter's eyes will look past mine.

It's time. We enter and I smooth her dress,
ease the veil down her soft flushed face.

Into the Woods

If a Romanian man kisses your hand, says
Your thigh curves like a river,
you can, if you wish,
step out of your life into a wood,
lie down among the bluebells
beside a rust coloured stream
made ripe with trout.
The taste of his blood will give you strength.
You could be anyone, say
I am only shadow, water follows me.
But if he asks: *What do you wish for?*
Will you say: *My life, just as it is?*

Cornmarket Street, Oxford

A gypsy grips you with her drooping eye.
She's pinned you to the wall, pressed
lavender under your nose.

For luck, she says as you rummage for coins.
Are you married? No.
Have you a good mother? Yes.

Take one for her too.
You've found two pounds, but she sees the mobile.
Give me three. Love will touch you again,

and there may be children. Her good eye knows she's
got you now.
Let me read your palm. But you're late. *I'm late.*

Let me put a crystal in your hand.
You're wavering.

The meeting is starting.

An Error of Timing

One morning
maybe you slept in.
Or there was a wedding
you forgot to attend.
Some small
error of timing
has brought you here
and you don't recognise
the colour of this stone.

Turn back,
ask directions of the man
selling melons
at the side of the road.
He doesn't know,
but says the melons are ripe.
The woman with the baby
signs to keep going
until you reach the sea.

Bridge

I got the clock, you the pots.
The only thing I wanted?
The small dish
blue as the sky over Prague,
its stumpy legs like udders.
Its markings orange as that café
the one with the tall proud hostess,
asparagus easy as butter,
where the air was still
nothing happened
and I thought only of your hands.

Wishing

The boat lay low, weighted
by young bodies which rocked
the dark lake each time they moved.

Above, they hoped, were stars
waiting to die and in that dying
yield up a wish for her, for him

for anyone out that August night.
The moon was half-full, half-empty.
Crickets played a persistent tune.

They were almost asleep and then –
a bright arc across the sky.
A dog barked, crickets paused.

They rowed back wide awake,
believing in wishes,
parting black water.

JOSEPH BUTLER

Joseph Butler was born in Oxford in 1962. He has earned a living as a farmer, teacher, blacksmith and boat-builder. 'Shoeing Shed' was first published by Two Rivers Press. 'Drawing Down' was first published in *Oxford Magazine*.

Opening Up

Even the key was his work,
the bow brazed to the stock,
the wards hand-filed and rivetted
so not-quite-perfectly,
so hair's breadth loose
you had to fish in the deadlock
for the leverage that slipped the bolt.

And the sense,
in the lift of the latch,
and the scuff of the timbers over the kerb,
of breaking a seal.
The forge unstoppered:
a tarry antiseptic breath
of woodsmoke and extinguished coals,
taste of steel like blood in the nostrils,
the seep of damp through undressed stone.

A clatter of daylight
over the sill,
and the breath indrawn.
In the gloom
the hunch of the hearth,
a crouch and a stillness of bellows,
folds roofed with dust,
soused-supple with linseed.
Their pumping-handle,
ashwood grain palmed smooth with use,
cranes forward,
considers.

The whole place appraising.
I feel myself weighed.
A judgement
made, withheld, deferred.
And into it
my own voice pitched,
a tremor in the air:
Have faith.
This is no trespass.

Moonlight

For four nights,
by a hunter's moon
you worked
the patch of ground
behind the forge.

You hoed along the lines of
cauliflowers and cabbages
whose plump hearts
folded to themselves
the dewy darkness.

You earthed the roots of your potatoes,
plied water from the rain-butt
to the wigwam-frame of runner beans.
Their rustling shivered upwards
to the stars.

Now couch grass overruns the plot.
I rake away the bindweed
and the bramble,
work the spade's edge down
between the nettles and the dock.

Beneath their roots
the soil is opalescent, finely tilthed.
It's crumbed
with horses' dung
and moonlight.

Wilfred

Mid-morning.
I glanced up from the fire
to the shock of his scrutiny:

his body hunkered in the doorway,
hunched and sparrow-slight,
his knuckles blueing on the upright of the frame.

He watched hungry as a boy,
but I felt my every movement weighed
against the stock of memory

his frame contained;
and knew myself clumsy, coltish,
the blows snatched, their aim misplaced.

Only when he'd gone
did the rhythm return:
cautious as a startled horse,

but workaday and powerful;
haltered in the compass of his vision,
in its reach and in its fading.

Shoeing Shed

That evening
I lit a candle in the shoeing shed,
in the place

he'd stooped and sweated,
lifted hooves
to brand the horn with slippery steel.

It burned all night,
puddled wax
in the channels of the cobbled floor.

It was summer
and the white froth of nettle
flowers craned in at the window;

columbine and vetch
trailed their stems
the length of the metal rack.

In the cemetery
the swallows skirled and feinted
through the cypress shelter-belt.

The clod I tossed into the grave
was warm, husked with sunlight.
It shattered on the coffin-lid.

Gifthorse

It was chanced upon,
unlooked-for:
a roadside happenstance,
a found poem.

Four stone walls and a wooden lean-to;
the space behind it snagged
with bramble, dogrose.

Water seeped from a rain-butt,
furled damp around a grindstone.
Creepers choked the furrows of the roof.
The glass panes filmed like cataracts.

I've never had the gift
of trusting providence.
Between my seeking and the finding
there've been gaps
too full of chanciness.
So when the sought-for thing appears
I look at it askance.

Through a fracture in the casement
you could see
the rust-bloom on an anvil,
the cowling of a brick-built hearth.
And still I doubted.
Nosed the smithy
as a creature would a trap.

As though the bleached wood of the lintel
might buckle, sag,
the chimney jolt,
and render back to brick.
As though the mortar of the place
might leach away,
and those
untenanted stones collapse.

Within the walls
the bellows at the fire's back
sighed.

Dead Men

I am warded by dead men,
guided by ghosts;
their touch on my arm is deft –
I fear for the skill in my hands.

I take his tools down from the rack
and watch
as the scroll coils,
the steel draws down.
The drift sinks plumb-centre
through the body of the bar.

These things are gifted:
I step into their spell.

In the upswing of the hammer
the blow's intuition.
In the pressure of my knuckles on the tongs
a nicety of angles judged.
As though their palms had printed on the place
a knowledge-hoard
that's mine to touch.

And at its heart the fire,
the cave of coals
through which the bellows' pulsing soughs.
Behind the suck-and-push of leather
I hear the sibilance of heat
that spreads along the bar.
The looseness that precedes the burning,
the lucent dangerousness of steel,
the hiss of their companionship.

Ammonite

As a child I watched
the peel and splinter of slate
as you picked in the cliff face
for fossils.

Something beautiful about the coils
that you dislodged,
their corrugations clenched across millennia,
stranded in a sea-bed turned to rock
that reared above the sand we stood upon.

Something fantastical, even then
about the sense you made of time,
the gaps it spanned
and their inversion
of the solid and the liquid things.

And something precious in the sand
whose gold grain ran a thread
between the old sea and the new,
the stone sea and the wind-ruffed
restless charge of water-onto-land.

You lent me your hammer to play with.
Its weight in my hand, the swing of it
too large,
its bounce and skew discarded,
abandoned on a rock.

Back at the car your anger rushed like water,
gathered the horizon to itself
and took me, rolled me over;
spun the world, and shattered on the tarmac.
Left me bloodied, breathless, still as stone.

And I remember how you ran,
with no thought but the hammer,
back across the beach
to beat the tide,
your footsteps flailing in the sand.

Drawing Down

It's the teasing out of stories
from blunt stock.
The refinement of endings.

Take a strand of steel and
heat it till the crystals' mesh unknits;
then compress

the livid end between the downward shock
of hammer-blow,
the counter-force

that is the anvil's weight:
the sheer, unmoving mass of it.
The physics say that softness yields

and elongates.
You feel its stretch through hammer's head
and hammer shaft –

the grain a telegraph to left-side brain,
the left hand knurled upon the stock
to centre and align

the bar beneath the blows.
And steel is sinuous,
not cast as liquid

but dislodged
towards a rearrangement, thinning out.
It's drawn down to a vanish-point

where blows run out on silence,
unsounded, and unnecessary.
The point made.

MARGARET EASTON

Margaret Easton was born in 1951 and grew up in Warwickshire. She studied English at the University of East Anglia. She works as a psychotherapist and lives in Suffolk.

Some of the poems in this anthology have appeared in *Oxford Magazine*, *Reactions* 3 and *Smiths Knoll*.

Laughing in Caves

I sat on the edge of my bed
cut clean into myself.
A clean cut, that's what I thought
would deal with my old self.

My job now is angels
for the drop-in paper-chain.
The trick with crepe is
keep the scissors steady
and don't stop.

I've painted the square pond
when fish slept under the ice.
You and me melted air holes
whispering, 'You mustn't wake up
mustn't, you'll die of cold.'

Apparently, routinely
frontier people cleared out forest
seeded in the shelter of their walls.
And stones never ran out
frost forces them up, even boulders.

Prayer flags freeze stiff.
The rock Buddha is up to his elbows
in offerings and snow.
A monk laughs in his cave
countless bright prayers in the blizzard.

Sitting on my bed with my old self
we go over all these things
under my breath, just until the ice breaks.
Any day now. Any day.

Sheltered

I miss climbing stairs, coal, lilac by the ditch.
I save pills in eggcups, my name is down on lists
for lunch, for baths, for an outing to the receding beach.

I get up, it's dull waiting, I wish He'd carry me off.
Again and again I disappear, I'm found
at the difficult junction opposite the post office

where I am on a list. I'm after the lilac I tell them
think of wood-pigeons building in the stand of pine,
banisters, I want to lay the fire. Irretrievable beach

banked up by bulldozers, poor nervy sandpipers
without enough shingle, ugly broken cliff
fenced off, poking with gorse root, ends of piping.

There are plenty of us, not free to disappear,
sat high in the minibus, each with a light raincoat,
all set. Trying to forget a ditch of lilac.

Tiggy's Tea

I am still waiting for a piece of fish, since yesterday.
They padlock switches.
I was sharp as glass once.
I manage the window with a toasting fork.
I know the chest of drawers, brooch, slippers.
I don't know here.
If it is Saturday they'll be up down, then straight out,
banging. They leave meals.
I get my people mixed up on the mantelpiece.
Mostly I'm afraid of being emptied out.
They knotted Union Jacks to my sticks
and we all got a tin of biscuits.
Prince Philip calls *her* Sausage.
Is this mine? I can eat crust.
Really, I am just here until I'm ready to go home.

Confirmation Day

Our dog bites so I patrol the lawn. Jeremy's come to borrow
    the guinea pig
his parents don't believe in pets. I show him my cross. I've
    been given
a red leather New Testament with ribbon book-mark attached,
    a white prayer-book
that must be covered in cellophane before it gets filthy mum says,
    and it's all well
and good Sally's mum going to march about the bomb but leaves
    her with the meringues.
Sally's got me to practise with old bread and a picnic mug of water.
    She's Catholic.
Wafer is cornet which I don't like because it sticks, but it's the body
    so I will, then wash it down.
My brother says prove it. Mum says there's far too much of all this
    at my school.
I'm to keep that cross in its box. Dad will hand out hymn books
    from the trolley.
We all have our maker to answer to, who sees everything.
    Sally's dad's
not going to church, he keeps to the back room where it's sunny,
    there's
a mantelpiece for his matchsticks, he adds them up, from the box
    to a pile
then back to the box then starts again. When he turns round his
    head's flat
sideways like the picture in my other Bible of a stone Egyptian.
    Once he cried.
Mum says it was the war, too late now, she can only hope, about
    those meringues.

Blood

Mine started in the games field lavs, like gum.
It couldn't be helped Miss Bates said, and sorted
me out in the sick room alcove which seemed
rude under the plaster of paris Holy Family.
I shan't tell the boys ever, I'll just yell
you've guessed wrong and slam my door.
Not like Poppy's sister, tells anybody,
it's a celebration she goes, and dances
pagan on the back lawn. She says worrying
about cold wash, soak and making a parcel
to burn in private is provincial.
Gina faints in assembly then has to be taken
out through the fire exit. It's made me
disorderly and full of excuses, apparently.
Perhaps if my mother could go easy, I mean
it's getting like with Stella last Whitsun.
The police found her at Great Malvern
on the back of Tim's motorbike.
Mysteriously ready, according to our Herbal.
I've bought a diary pencil with a rubber
so I can move the crosses.

Exposures

I like looking at pictures. After the illness I was given a duffle coat,
brown with a hood I always wore. I was sent photographs I got lost in.
A picture of me with my hood up looking out from the warm, rough
    covering,
looking out from the fearfulness we all come from and I had been
    returned to.
On the top of the mountain sun and ice burn equally never defeating
    each other.
Perfect balance is always on its way to or from imbalance, otherwise
    there would be
only emptiness, no space, no speech. But the shining peaks can be
    merciless.

I am not ready yet for the company of lichen. In the foothills which
    I prefer
is a patch of sunlight, of ice, of moss. I move from one to the other
    between
the shade of spruce and larch, the scent of flowering thyme stirred
    by the short,
intense search of butterflies, the astonishing quiet of cowslip and
    winter aconite.
All over the mountains are paths trodden to doors of chapels where
    villagers have left
food for hermits. The holy is work. Monks come chanting with
    recorders and
tambourines, they travel from wide, dry places of Asia Minor
    through
valleys of stone eating only figs and rare herbs. A brown contour
    of song,
one part always out of sight in a bend of the path. Wherever I
    stand I shall
only catch a part of the song. Goatherds converse by whistling
    from one hillside
to the next. Not just instructions, whole conversations pass the
    time of day
through miles of fresh air. Keeping in touch, that's what it's
    about, I haven't
been out now for fourteen years, but I know these things happen,
    I keep in touch.

HELEN FARISH

Helen Farish is publishing her first collection, *Intimates*, with Jonathan Cape. She is completing a doctoral thesis on the poetry of Sharon Olds and Louise Glück. She also teaches literature and creative writing. In 2003 she was awarded a grant from Arts Council England, South-East.

Poems in this anthology have been previously published in *Tying the Song*: Poetry School anthology 2000, *Oxford Magazine*, *PN Review* and *Feminist Review*.

Look at These

Seeing you makes me want to lift up my top,
breathe in and say *Look! Look at these!*
I've kept them hidden till now
under loose shirts, Dad's jumpers.

Suddenly I'm offering them
like a woman ready to mate.
I'm holding my breath.
Don't tell me not to.

Here is a Leopard

of ivory, coral and copper.
See how strong it is, how certain.

Such a creature knows its way in life,
gives up the chase if appropriate.

It is probably the finest
gift you will ever receive.

I estimate it will take you
the best part of a lifetime to agree.

When I danced with you at the Knights' Palace
people stopped dead in their tracks to watch.

Auto Reply

As Jesus went on from there, he saw a man named Matthew sitting
at the tax collector's booth. 'Follow me', he told him, and Matthew
got up and followed him.

On my desk I left a reminder
of what to buy for supper, a scummy
mug of tea, unanswered

emails, no out-of-office
auto reply. I left bank accounts
open, my part-time degree

in piles. I left clothes drying
on the kind of creamy autumnal day
that brings seagulls in from the coast.

I'd fantasised about such a thing thinking
it would take the form of falling
for a woman. I remember how easily

I used to well up – an advert
in which the sea was slowed down
or that movie line: *always be·yourself.*

Looking back it's clear
something had risen to the top.
You walked by, skimmed it off.

Alcyone and Ceyx

It was your leather jacket.
When you left the room I would smell it,
longing to let my hands loose on you,
lust like pub smoke clinging to me.

My father said how could his daughter
love someone with a motorbike,
who drank pints, wore ear-rings?
He warned me what Zeus would do.

I was made a halcyon, you a diver,
our nest wrecked with every tide.
Then out of the blue the sea
still enough for eggs to hatch.

I hate the sky and the water,
the good clean life they smell of.
I long for your leather jacket,
my dress blown tight against me.

What Held Us There

They made everyone's heart sing, the folk dancers
with their raggedy band. We were all looking

for an excuse to linger: Saturday morning,
the market, the good feeling wind.

I would have said it was spring, that feeling,
but the summer was well through, almost

looking back on itself. And that was what held us there
though we didn't know it, that we were looking back

on ourselves, the market, the raggedy band,
the singing inside just there and then.

Feathered Coyote

Your ancestors called prostitutes
'bringers of happiness'.
I bring you happiness.

I go to another bed, you follow me,
pull back the sheets, look at me
as though I am a mythical creature,

flowers being made from my hair,
fine grass from my skin.
The *coyote emplumado*

has followed me home from the museum
with an appetite to be the labeller
not the labelled.

Yesterday you called me wife,
amor, chaparrita.
Now my label is the oldest there is

and when you say it in your language
I perform it in mine.
You lie back, feathers everywhere.

Mount Mirtagh and Back

The emperor Qianlong was obsessed with jade.
To recover the finest boulder from Mount Mirtagh
he sent 1000 men, 100 horses.

Bridges had to be built, mountain paths carved,
in the tender rain roads cut through bluish forests,
and in winter water was frozen for ice-slides.

I want to be like that boulder.
I want bringing me back now to cost you.
I want the irony of how there was a time

I'd have cut the road myself
never to be lost on you,
how there was a time

if my black slip smelt of both of us
I treated it like imperial green jade.
Send me a leaf-shaped agate cup and a thousand

heart-shaped promises. Say you were a fool
to let me slip through your fingers
like water refusing to freeze.

And should the ground ever soften
I'll ask if you remember that first time
you passed me the agate cup saying you would gladly

become a tree, wait all winter to grow a leaf
tender enough to touch my lips.
And in my heart-shaped space then I swore

that for you I'd go to Mount Mirtagh and back
without knowing even where it was
nor how willing you'd be to send me.

Newly Born Twins

In separate incubators one of the twins was dying.
Against doctor's orders, a nurse put them together.

The strong twin, the one with nothing
pulling her back, she slung
her newly born arm over
the one who was wanting to leave,
and stabilised her heartbeat, made everything
regular in the body of the one who'd already
had enough.

The strong one, she will think
she is God, that she can pull back
life from where it was wanting to go.
It will be harder for her
than for the one who already knows
about separation, loneliness, where
they can make you want to go.

Surgery

That woman who chose to have her breasts removed
rather than live with the fear of cancer
woke up to a flat
bandaged chest,
her body saying *but why*
when I hadn't turned against you?

Like a surgeon
I sever you. Mutilation
or preventative medicine – I'll never know.
But preferable the flat half of the bed
to your hand on my breast one night, the next
on someone else's.

Mesoplodon Pacificus

I have shown myself to you
only as drift and you have presumed
to deduce me from this.

I routinely descend
into abysmal depths,
am far from land, secretive.

But what do you know of my breach,
how the lightless world
bursts off me –

how I can feed on this
for thousands of miles,
the routine weight of air crushing

the sea's surface suddenly
gone, suddenly
an opening into which I pour.

Mesoplodon Pacificus: a species of whale known to exist only because of 'drift' (stranded specimens).
A 'breach' is when the whale clears the surface of the sea in a spectacular jump.

China Dogs

I could think about my mother's sister:
a tea-table to be cleared to the tick
of the monkey clock, jams back

to the pantry, bank up the fire;
outside a bitter Easter and the stretched-out
slowness of life. That's what I could do:

find passageways back to rooms
where afternoons sit quiet as china dogs
and evening comes easy as late snow.

Give me china dogs
to hold onto, I say, let no one
drop me.

The Old King's Gardens

I love you now like I love
unswept paths, unkept groves, like I love
the elegant old hothouse where nothing

will ever grow again, the place an emblem
of pleasure gone by. I couldn't
begin with you all over. What I felt

has acquired the dream-like quality
of those light-thin curtains,
their yearning in the breeze.

Plum Island

Even as I was parking and looking
at the backs of people on the dune I knew

they'd seen something, the way they
held themselves like the chosen ones.

And I had driven up
late in the day, empty-handed,

as though I could see this anytime:
this acreage of ocean uncrashing, slowed

by the thick coat of day on its back.
Was I half way through life and unprepared

for abundance, for noiseless
waves unscrolling?

KELLY GROVIER

Kelly Grovier was born in the United States and was educated at the University of California, Los Angeles. He came to the United Kingdom to study Romanticism after being awarded Fulbright and Marshall scholarships for postgraduate research. At present, he is completing a doctoral thesis on the eighteenth-century adventurer and philosopher 'Walking' Stewart at Christ Church, Oxford. He is an editor of the literary magazine *Oxford Poetry* and a regular contributor to *The Times Literary Supplement*. His poems have previously appeared, or are forthcoming, in several publications including *Poetry Review*, *Quadrant* (Australia, ed. Les Murray), the *May Anthologies*, and the *Oxford Magazine*.

Of the poems appearing in this anthology, only one has previously been published: 'The Recipe', which first appeared in the *Oxford Magazine*.

The Recipe

Calls for thirty years of fear.
Chin trembles in an empty street
For no apparent reason.
It calls for sweating
When someone unexpectedly
Makes reference to you-
Know-what, and a short
Sharp needle jab in the side
Of your neck when the phone

Rings. A train rumbles
Past and all of its freight
Doors are open facing you.
You recognise the cargo
As it passes by one
Car at a time. Father
Mother brother son.
When the rain begins to fall
You try to separate

The strands like a bead curtain,
But start slipping on the glass
Sliding under your feet.
At first, your calves hurt,
And your thighs, but after
A while you forget about
The pain and spend your time
Trying to remember what it was
The recipe called for next.

Camping Out

The infinite regression of things
Was never made clearer to you
Than that starless night
When you took the form
Of a chattering chicken's head
Projected onto the nylon
Wall of a tent, and looking back

At the pinched forefinger and thumb
That made your beak, back
Through the clenched middle and ring
Fingers to the flickering
Kerosene lantern, you knew that even he,
Your pudgy, rotten-toothed, dim-
Witted creator, could not behold what

You, a knuckle-brained silhouette
Could see on the other side
Of the screen: the racoon at the picnic
Basket, the speckled fawn disappearing
Under brush for fear, and beyond
The timberline, the fat orange moon
That was busy obliterating the stars.

The Metal Clasp

On your leather satchel squeaks
Every time you take a step
As though a small bird
Were following behind you.
In the coming darkness
The fog grazes at your ankles

Like a flock of lost sheep
And you recognise the black one
From tricks the trees used to play
Outside your bedroom window.
When the shepherd comes
Over the midnight mountains

His face full of the moon
You drop your shears to see
What it is he holds
In his outstretched hands –
The silver feathers and the beak –
Still quiet in his palms.

The Ancient of Days

That summer, I was the broken
Clock on the old church tower
In the little village square.
Pigeons would gather beneath me
And I would mark the passage
Of time by the length
Of their shadows, the rhythm

Of their ritual dance. With teeth
Clenched and hands
Frozen on the hour of a death –
Unable to relinquish
Even a minute – I compassed
Silently in the air arranging
The universe into angles

And calibrating the wavelengths
Of stars, while behind me,
On the other side of the wall,
With his arms stretched out straight
For eternity, staring at an empty
Cup, there was another, who was hell-
Bent, trying to disprove me.

The Ledger

In which you record the names
Of those responsible. Your great-
Grandfather whose blurred black-
And-white face got warped
By rain when the glass cracked.
The uncle with the one arm
And the niece who died in
Childbirth everyone always said

Looked just like you. A pluck
Of a string like music
To a spider's ear who knows
By the merest vibration of floss
Which quadrant of his spun harp
A thing has come to die in. Beyond
The webbed window, a fawn
Inspects her spots in the pale light

Of the full moon and your mind
Becomes your fingers fumbling
With something folded in your pocket.
A prescription you never returned for;
The name is yours, and the signature,
But you don't recognise the writing
As you begin copying each syllable
Onto the next line of the ledger.

JOHN MASON

John Mason was born in 1952 and grew up between the middle-class values of the diplomatic service and the rich variety of life abroad. After public school and Cambridge, where he read Modern and Medieval Languages, an invitation to teach at Christ's Hospital started him on a career in education. For many years he lived in the Welsh Marches, working in education, in forestry and in arts administration, while continuing to write and collaborate with composers and artists. He now lives in Denmark, teaching at the University of Southern Denmark.

A collection *From the Black Square*, accompanied by a large collection of watercolours by Peter Horrocks, appeared in 1984. The poems in this anthology have not previously been published.

The Last Elm in England

It was the last elm in England, though no one knew it then.
In our young days we had made love in its shade
And after, lying satisfied, traced its branching hierarchies
Against the passing clouds. Its rootedness was a comfort
That held the birds in symmetry around its crown
As it held our children swinging in long arcs
Across the lawn or climbing up into their pirate den.
Their grandmother's footsteps could have been my own,
My mother's, hers, the shadows playing hide-and-seek.
And then, one after-summer afternoon, it started to speak.

The children heard it first, their arms round its trunk, their ears
Pressed to its hollows. 'It's whispering!' they whispered.
Its surfaces were thick with moths, struggling over the bark,
Their bodies black and snub, their wings flexing and crackling
    like sails.
It was the first sign. There were others. Round an old burr,
Fungus formed a collar. Bark hung loose. Small fingernails
Prised open a parasite world that fled towards the dark.
Together we watched the birds feast, the leaves crumple like
    hands
That were tired of giving. I showed them the tell-tale band
Of death under the bark. 'Wicked!' was all they said.

They watched from an upstairs window the tree's dismembering.
One by one the branches were swung down on ropes and flung
To the fire, till only the trunk was left. Piecemeal the chainsaw
Segmented it to logs that crashed on the lawn and shook the house.
When it was done, a stillness gathered, a blank remembering,
A shadow ghosted against the overcast sky. In dreams that night
    I saw
My children as trees. Birds played in their hair while the sun shone.
But in the gathering dark their voices fell silent, their songs,
And I watched them wither, crying 'Water!' with black swollen
    tongues,
The moths crackling in their mouths, their throats, their lungs.

The Last of the Islanders

On clear days we could see the mainland on the horizon like a fur
    of mould,
But for the most our cliffs wept in a mist that caught at the lungs,
Made uncles cough like sheep and blanketed our incests in its folds.
In the reek of salt fish and peat smog, we grew up stained and strong.
Our women's hands, lanolined smooth as soap with fleece and
    plaited dough,
Kneaded on the same grained deal where we gave birth and died.
Our laird left us alone. In the tallow light, as the battered radio
Ebbed and hissed with the tide, we cleaned our teeth on tough husks
    of rye,
Learned of the storms we lived among and sized up the purpose
In our elders' eyes. Their wishes were a ballast to our prayers,
Weighted our pillows with an acrid scent, pointed our dreams like a
    compass.
Our knowledge was the island of our fathers. Nothing was unfamiliar
Until the woman, embarking on the jetty, laughed and handed out
    lollipops,
Made smoke from the school-house chimney and chalked our names
    on slate.
At first we kept our distance. On her map, the island was a full-stop,
Its sky unclouded, waves becalmed and the mainland across a hairline
    strait
Was vast as the sea. Our elders told us what we knew. She lied.
Yet the island was uneasy. We shut our doors, refused her milk and fuel,
But still we heard her singing, saw her brightly coloured clothes hung
    out to dry,
Watched each week the mail-boat unload novelties as dangerous as
    jewels –
A bicycle with gears, a gramophone, a television set.
It was this last that tipped the balance. Stationed on her window-sill,
It had our noses pressed to the uncurtained glass, motionless as limpets,
While the Saint's white Volvo sped away, or the Lone Ranger reared
    on Silver.
It was weeks before she noticed us. When the snow began to settle
    in our hair,
She called us in. With shuffling feet and mugs of steaming cocoa
We stood wide-eyed, transfixed, and came again. It was the end of an era.
Our houses shrank, grew cold and grimed; the words our elders spoke

Burned on our cheeks; their customs we thought archaic, later even
    a crime.
Our teacher gave us ears for the world. We heard its call and answered.
Each hoisted his kit-bag aboard and leaning on the rail saw the
    coastline climb
Into view, the future swim towards him like a legendary bird.

The Merchant Tailor

The merchant tailor, widowed thirteen years, smoothes back his bolt
And feels its shining. The weft contains no sun. Its warmth is counterfeit.
He knew some fabrics – skin or consonant – surrendered easy,
    hardened to a fault
And threw the dye. May rain streaks the glass, trickles over the slate.
The gutters, choked again, fill to overflow.

Stippled with blue light, the starling on the ridge stabs at a cropped
Button of jade moss. The sheen explodes in its beak, sheer velvet
Torn. How she complained, come spring, at the mess they dropped
Like words, like mutes – the guttersnipes. Yesterday he saw the nest,
Woven makeshift, shapeless,

Housing four scarlet tongues, fragile silken aspirants,
Pronouncing consonants in a crown. She was too soft of skin
To bear. Her breath unravelled till earth stopped her silences.
The wasps this year are early. His fingers, waxy with the nap of cloth,
    begin
To smooth its wings, again, again.

ANN PHILLIPS

Ann Phillips was educated at a grammar school in Kent, her home county, and at St Hilda's College, Oxford. In spite of the Oxford connection she is a long-term resident of Cambridge. She first worked in publishing, part of the time at Cambridge University Press, and then changed course and worked at Newnham College, Cambridge, in several different capacities – finally as the college's archivist.

She has edited texts of Milton and Shakespeare, and an anthology of reminiscences for Newnham, and has had five novels for young readers published by Oxford University Press.

She has only recently started to have poetry published, apart from words set to music. Of the poems included here, 'Depths' and 'Wings' have appeared in *Camcophony*, a Cambridge anthology.

Raindance

The rainmakers dance, man and woman,
making the rain, man and woman.
First they make the rain's feet
shuffling as if they paddled through puddles
kicking as if they kicked off water.

They dance the rain's legs, man and woman,
striding and standing, rain in straight pillars.
They dance the rain's body, swaying and shaking,
solid and steady rain, the world's goodness,
hour by hour, day by day, monthly and yearly.

They dance the rain's arms, man and woman,
flailing and tossing their hands with spread fingers
wrists working as the rain comes on gusts in windstorms.

They bow their heads and draw circles above their necks
to make the rain's head, man and woman.
The rain's face may not be looked at and must not be imagined.
If it is scowling floods will scour the valleys
sweeping off cattle and children.

But they twiddle their fingers above their heads, man and woman,
to make the rain's hair which is spray and drizzle.

They piss, up and down, man and woman,
to make the rain's genitals.
Rain must have babies:
its children are rivers and irrigation channels
bush and blossom and seed-corn.

When they have danced, man and woman,
drums echo their feet
first a soft pitter-patter
next rattling downpour
then thump of thunder.

When the dance is over people go apart, man and woman,
to make love, make babies.
The wells will be full for them.

When no rain comes with the moon's increase
and no rain comes with the moon's decrease
who can tell – perhaps the creature of rain was laughing
and it comes down richly now in some other country.

Company

Let them come, comers
It is the hour of Matins
  These two will come together
  beginning at the beginning
    They will bring tapers and lamps
    sugar mice and oranges
    the harsh dark will be alight
    with a bloom like plum-dust
  I shall not hear them go or come
  They hold the roof-tree steady

Let her come, Margaret Ruth
It is the hour of Lauds
  time for the early one
  whose chime was quickly muffled
    She will bring an opened rose
    for me to tell the colour
    She will come barefoot
    who never wore shoes or stockings
  She lays down the doorsill

Let them come, Louie and George
It is the hour of Prime
    They will bring butter and milk
    cups and plates that never match
    a hymnbook (texts without the tunes)
    and a scent of hay and orchards
    the ring and the rattle of wagons and hooves
  They put the stone foundations

Let them come, Lizzie and Fred
It is the hour of Terce
        They will bring biscuits and salt
        red Venetian vases
        a Bible and a pack of cards
        mouthfuls of pithy sayings
        the running of water and creak of boats
    They put the bricks and mortar

Let them come, Hally and Ron
It is the hour of Sext
        They will bring wild flowers
        a manual on the British bats
        their collective lore on footpaths
    They set the doors, wide open

Let them come, Aura and May
It is the hour of Nones
        They will bring books of songs
        invention of stories and of names
        garnets, a waft of orris-root
    They set the windows, breathing

Let them come, Jo, Flora, Pauline
It is the hour of Vespers
        They will bring garden plants and books
        the songs on the river and the swans
        the dancing to mark the first of May
    They put the slates on for me

Let them come, four-pawed ones
It is the hour of Compline
        They will bring nothing but will purr
        around the bed till dawning
        and carpet the house with their shed fur
    a house empty of mourning

Rose Petals

Opening the wardrobe door, I am caught again
by the blurred scent of rose petals and skin
My clothes hang limp as the dead
and one fine pleated shirt, bone colour, stands out
formal as a shroud

When do we see them now, the sheeted dead?
They go out of the back door with the men in black
without the viewing and wake
without the lilies and candles at foot and head
and the ceremonial cake

I remember her in her nightgown, one day old
I touch the mirror glass of the door   She wasn't cold
the July child, but half warm
like an egg not long laid
like a small fallen plum in the long grass and deep shade

Nor was she marble white but a waxy grey
the rosebud put in her fingers gone flat and blue
The loss of a sister can never be put away
I shut the boxwood door, but without relief
from the death of the child who taught my childhood grief

Wings

> 'With twain it covered its face
> and with twain it covered its feet
> and with twain it did fly'
> Isaiah 6.2

When their flame was flickering out
damped down by rising anger
seraphim chose to get rid of their insignia
        hack away shackles
and they gnawed or clawed off each other's wings

When the first pair fell
they saw each other naked to the feet
    surprised by the stir of possibility
    puzzled at being beasts of a not-yet-existent field

When the second pair fell
their feet hit ground
    they gasped with the shock to their unhardened heels

When the third pair fell
their eyes were not covered from the sight of God
    they looked up once
    then turned and ran for it
    (what they would have given for wings)

They did the six-minute mile and the marathon
They are still running and they daren't look back

Nothing will ever get rid of the bloodstains from their teeth and
    nails
or dry the oozing from their wounded shoulders

Depths

    This is where the wrecks are.
    Water moves little here, but it wafts the weed
    through gangways, portholes, and across the decks;
    and we have seen the bottom-most on chairs
    around the walls, open mouths, unseeing eyes.
    Don't be afraid. They can sing; they have been seen
    walking under water.

    This is where the treasure is:
    cargoes and jetsam, coelocanths, priceless shells,
    all kinds of finds not on record, imagined lost.
    Cities are ruined but their truths are not:
    the skilled make beauty of their brokenness.
    Things swim, to divers' eyes; statues have been seen
    walking under water.

This is where the timeless is.
Strange, as the sea sways always to moon and tide,
eternity is what we know it means:
where change is a changing back, and forgotten found.
The expected angels with their finny wings,
their round gold eyes, their scales, will at last be seen
walking under water.

CHRISTOPHER SOUTHGATE

Christopher Southgate was born in 1953. He trained originally as a research biochemist, finishing a Ph.D at Cambridge in 1977, and has since been a house-husband, a bookseller, and lay chaplain in a university and a hospital. He has published four collections of poetry, including a verse biography of T.S. Eliot (*A Love and its Sounding*, Salzburg, 1997) and *Beyond the Bitter Wind: Poems 1982–2000* (Shoestring, 2000). He was awarded a Hawthornden Fellowship in 1999. When not writing he lectures on the science–religion debate at Exeter University.

An earlier version of 'Taboo' appeared in The Company of Poets' anthology *Taboo* (Blue Button, 1993).

A Month after her Death

We are all experts on our memories.
I elide the blood-apricot moon of my mother's dying
with last night's yellow, jazz moon,
reorganise them like a chess defence,
a Grünfeld against grieving.
On every board but one
it works
       for I have made it hard
to spot the opening. A shy boy sees it,
remembers journeys,
                notices a Japanese magnolia
come into flower, hears the cadence
of being taught its Latin name.
I offer him my resignation, move from board to board,
flick clock after clock. The boy is too stubborn
to accept. He sets my defences upright,
destroys them again and again.

Taboo

*Otto Hahn and Lise Meitner collaborated on the experiments that led
to the discovery of nuclear fission in 1938–9.*

It is in our bones, in the knitting of them,
In the assembly of our atoms
Into community. Taboo was there in Eden.
For one fruit glowed with forbiddenness;
On one tree, plain enough perhaps
To look at, which in spring had flowered
Like an outbreak of stars, or in blossoms
Fine as a flamingo's wing, but then
Was ordinary in leaf, half-hiding
The wonderful harvest – on that one tree
We may imagine concentrated all
The chantment of a world made by God –
All the left-over star-stuff of the cosmogoner.

So that to eat the faintly glowing fruit
Was just to come a hair's breadth, a photon-burst too close
To the one who had formed all things. To be exposed
To a blast of possibility
Too vast to be contained within our frame.
Which we did, and have dealt since then –
Man to blamed woman, human to all
This glory-scattered planet – evil.

But what if the fruit
Revered, measured from an admiring distance,
Should then be found to fragment *of itself* –
To drip its star-stuff on the innocent?
It had been doing so for years, when Otto
Helped his Lise pack her bags for Sweden.

Even in the dull, static lab photo,
Two of them staring stiffly at the frame
From a suitable distance apart
You can see the respect, yes, but also
The intensity of their affection, Otto's
Sturdiness, Lise's passionate commitment –
Severe, brilliant, Jewish, banned.

He writes to her about her other luggage
And by the way that he – silly – cannot
Seem to separate product from carrier
In the tests on the slow-neutron block.
Poor man. He has put the answer into
The question, used a cider barrel to test
For apple-juice.
Lise, exiled from everything she knew,
Writes back – challenges, explains, confides
'A few private requests', especially
'My index card file'. She pushes him
To look clearly into the dark glass.
On an envelope he notes her suggestion
As to the energy release. That
Is the horror. And he cannot sleep,
And he cannot but – out here beyond
Eden, where there is no concealment –
Cannot but consider (knowing his species),

The taking of his own life.
For once we find the innermost kernel
Can be made to melt before our eyes
The world is filled with a deadly, tabooless searching,
Pressing life hard against the unmeltable sword.

Later, watching the neutrons do their work,
Brighter than the New Mexico sun, a man
Wrote that he had become death,
Quoting Krishna. We reinvoke our favourite
Myths to look for limits. The lovely world
Is full of dissipate enchantment
And of the toxins we have made of it –
To poison a lamb at two thousand miles,
To kill a river with a teaspoon's dose.

Bring on the myths, then, and let them play
In the violent sunsets of this man-fired world.
And let but one taboo remain –
Against the crushing of that respect
I see in Otto's photograph. The furled
Rose of love, unanatomised,
Allowed to be itself, the high meadow
Allowed its brief tossings of joy.
For thirty years they worked together,
Always staying late. When the chemistry went well
They would sing Brahms to each other.
And every night each
Walked back from the Institute alone.

Bring on the myths again, but let them never
Lose (worst mockery of all)
The sense of how love can suffer and forgive
And give its secrets up – from Stockholm
For a card file, from many Golgothas.
Releasing us – to play death with the whole
Soul-stuff of the world – or into peace,
The furrow worked as though a garden – the future
Hoped for, as though it might belong to God.

Marilyn and Joe DiMaggio

'Oh Joe, I sang to the boys in Korea.'
How he loved that breathlessness in her voice
and how she'd come to bed
wearing nothing but the Yankees hat
in which he'd hit fifty-six games straight
and won nine World Series.

'When I sang in Korea
you just can't believe
how people cheered.
Joe, you can't imagine.'

Arms flung in the air
then sending the hat skimming
into the closet.

How he wished she'd stretch her agile mind
past cult figures
and her own applause.
He'd known applause.
He only wanted love
and clear signals.

And he said,
'honey' –
the moment of making
the straightforward play,
the moment of the final out –
'honey, I think I can.'

Artist of the Island Sun

The day is used up now, and the sun falls.
Its worshippers wriggle their bodies away, and the deckchair man,
Who has seen everything, allows himself a moment
To consider the sea.

It develops a stripe of light, reddish, burnt gold,
Stretching from the west. As he thinks on this
The stripe draws in towards him,
Its colour deepens.

Where they suck back off the shingle
The waves clear a few feet of sand,
New-mint them in copper, more brilliant
Than a hero's shield-rim.

Now only the backs of the wave-crests glow
As they run in ever-changing mosaic
Across the blue-green ink
Of the sea,

Now only twenty waves find the light,
Crinkle it, grow a film of running cream;
Now only ten – will the day be saved
For a mere ten slivers of white-edged fire?

The deckchair man knows better.
He has foreseen it all – the last five waves
Surfaced with burning petrol, the shield-rim's
Glow extinguished.

The sun's final fall is a reactor in meltdown,
The Taj burning,
An ancient domed church
Turned to oil-lamp;

Lastly a circus tent that a slate-coloured cloud
Fails to hold, for all its ropes of crimson silk. The air smokes
With the onset of night. The man rests, turning eastward;
Trade dictates he give birth again tomorrow.

Riddle

A man with iron-grey hair and glasses
Contemplates the cedar tree in the grounds.
He is a grizzly bear
He is a lover under the Cyprus moon
He passes his days at sketching and poetry.

A man with iron-grey hair and glasses
Paces up and down in a basement room
Talking to himself. In his right hand
A small grey object, tightly clutched.
He tells it a story, stops, tells it again.

I pass the two of them in the car-park.
The first man greets me warmly,
Presses my hand. The second
Does not seem to recognise me
Although we have met often.

I ask them both how things are.
'Grim,' the first says. 'Miserable.'
The other (when pressed for an answer) 'Pretty grim.
They expect more and more from me,
Provide less and less.'

The two men talk once a week
At scheduled liaisons of ten resentful minutes.
The poet shouts, the other listens.
A sort of marriage exists between them.
Psychiatry is its name.

Reweaving the Rainbow

We have unwoven the glowing strands,
Seen hope as multiple internal reflection,
Measured indigo in Ångströms.

We know where to look for the Lord's sign –
Always opposite the sun, at a certain angle,
The double bow above, and fainter,
(Reversed, of course, since the light
As though losing its way on a roundabout
Performs an extra pass of the rain's geometry.)

Knowing where to look

Take a handful of soil from under a loved tree,
Or dip your hands in a bowl of rosewater
Tinctured with yew;

Make the mark of the bow on a friend's hand.
Trace the seven colours of love there –
Sense, fainter, what, between friends,
Can never be spoken.
Feel the elements within you
Stir towards the glow of freedom.

In Front of Chagall's 'Americas Window'

Eyes rest, dissolve into a deep
Lucid blue, like a lead-lined
Mosaic of the sea at nightfall.

Eyes play on a primitive mouth
At a trumpet, a lifted gold megaphone
Out of a riot of blue.

A child of America stumbles at the tripwire.
For an instant the arc of her balance
Crosses Chagall's cascading light,

Points to the field-grey of the courtyard.
Leaded blue and luminous violet tumble together,
Buckle the upraised torch of liberty.

The child and the masterpiece are saved
By an arresting hand. The arc remains,
Printed on us as possibility.

JULIAN STANNARD

Julian Stannard was born in 1962 and was educated at the universities of Exeter and Oxford. He has taught at both the University of Genoa and Suffolk College, a college of the University of East Anglia. He is the author of *Rina's War* (Peterloo Poets, 2001), poems from which appeared in *First Pressings* (Faber) and the *Guardian*. He has also written a study of Fleur Adcock entitled *From Movement to Martians* (Edwin Mellen, 1997) and has published widely in magazines and journals in Britain, Ireland and USA. His work has recently been translated and published in *Resine* (Italy).

Of the poems in this anthology 'Peace' was first published in *Reactions* 2, 'The Red Zone' in *Reactions* 3 and 'Tuesday' in *Reactions* 4. 'A Box of Cigars' appeared in *Smiths Knoll* and 'Blue Shoe' first came out in the *London Magazine*.

The Red Zone

I need to get back into the Red Zone
because I left something in the apartment
ten, twenty, thirty years ago.
And this little row of pants lining the alleyway,
handwashed, sparkling…
I need to climb these slate stairs.
Has anyone bothered with the locks?
And I thought the city so quiet
until helicopters drifted over my shoulder.
I need to get into that apartment
with its high ceilings, its whorey curtains,
the bat still flapping in the wardrobe,
a baby on the table.
Did someone leave a baby on the table?

Peace

Our lives passed by in a state of desire.
Narrative of rubble, sob-shake of stones.
We hopped off trams, arranged the rendezvous.
The Tommies were kind but aloof, and the Yankees!
We loved the French for their manners.
One night we tampered with the wires for light.
There was no poverty under bedclothes.
The city was our children's kindergarten.
They grew up in six days with quick eyes.
One night we spilt champagne over a dress.
The city tottered, the elderly tottered.
Speeches of the Führer were sold under arches.
Ghosts were blown in with the dust.
Dust was blown in with the ghosts.

A Box of Cigars

That flag stood for Britain, remember?
We owned a map and coloured it red,
the ramifications were ghastly.

These were our colonial villas,
these were our kind loyal servants
who did not come back to our world.

Who knows what happened to them?
Bad enough what happened to us:
we grew old and died and got mixed up

in other people's lives. Only the Coghills
stayed on – rubber was it?
Alas, it didn't work out. It rarely does.

But in this box of cigars which
is home to a collection of beautiful faces
I can still look through banisters

and see a room of people I somehow know
dressed up immaculately in the heat
all skirting round a tray of drinks.

Blue Shoe

One leg neatly crossed over the other.
On the end of mother's foot a blue shoe,
it perched there like a bird on a tree.
Every time she moved it creaked…

With the slightest twitch of a toe
the room sounded like a galleon:
lurching water, groaning wood.
A blue shoe, a blue ocean, political

discourse howling with blueness.

The Mill at Tidmarsh

I want to swim at the Mill at Tidmarsh.
I will take a really big breath and go down deep
I might even start to drown a little
and then come up in a hurry, flapping my arms
as I suddenly break clear of the water.
Or I might even decide to stay a wee bit longer.
But then I'll shake myself down
naked, cocky, white as paper…
And I'd certainly shout out something like
'It's paradise! Why don't you come in?'
and Lytton would pretend not to peep.
I hesitate. Will I ever be brave enough to do this again?
The water's cold but perfect.
The weeds are baring their teeth.

Tuesday

This simple idea
of living in a house.
I like brick walls
that measure off a garden,
the way a greenhouse
occupies a lawn,
it really is a most vulnerable temple.
I like its clean shake of glass
and a voice is telling me
that the crooling of a dove
is a train before
it comes into shunting.

GREG SWEETNAM

Greg Sweetnam was born in Canada in 1959, of Irish parents. He studied graphics at Berkshire College of Art and Design and currently commissions book design and illustration for an educational publisher. He has a daughter and lives in Oxford with his wife Polly.

'Mother is always there' was first published in *Cyphers*. 'Sketch' appeared in *Island City* (Broad Street Poetry, 1999), an anthology of Oxford poems by living Oxford poets, edited by Rip Bulkeley.

Sculptor's Child

Before he carves his own keepsake he looks
Into himself and touches the site
Then sets to it with his mallet's bluntness

Driving the chisel, opening space, a stone
Lighter. Now he is younger, slimmer,
His old self. Tapping at the temple again

He is answered by a small collapse
But keeps a firm grip on the struck probe,
Unsettled and unsettling.

It's clear to him, the shape he was in
Before he had the knowledge to shape himself,
And now his dwindling body has reached that point

It is a boy's eyes that stare as he works
At the head, the line of the jaw, the curve
Of the cheek, the delicate nose and ears,

Stopping at the uncut mouth, the open
Mike of the chisel in his hand going close
Or as close as he dares.

Mother is always there

Mother is always there
In the morning before school.
She is there after school.

Mother is always there
In snapshots out of focus,
Her hands on our shoulders.

Mother is always there,
Holds a box, tight with matches
For her forty filtered tips.

Mother is always there
With my father in the kitchen
Where they go to clear the air.

Mother is always there,
Keeling over into chairs;
Stoned on Doctor's orders.

Mother is always there
At the weekend, home for rest
From five days spent in care.

Mother is always there
In her chair, sitting still,
At a loss for anything.

Mother is always there
At the end of the river
Which takes her by the feet.

Mother is always there:
Why does Father never talk
About her to the boys?

Terrestrial

Beyond the troubled water, a tablespoon
Of oil was warming in a pan. A blue flame.
I turned up the oven, anticipating
The smell, sight, touch and taste. A grateful palate,
As though my tongue had opened a channel.

A sound came through: a TV for company
In the next room. The opening of *Lifelines*
After the news and weather showed a woman
Given to wondering why she hadn't drowned,
Watching her double put her self through it

This drama played out once more for the camera
In a flooded car, parked on the riverbed.
I sat close, so drawn to her I held my breath
As she unclipped her belt and kicked off her shoes
And pulled herself through the snaggle-toothed windscreen.

She spoke with the air of rapid thought balloons
As she rose, lured towards the face lit by blue
Aquarium light, of the boy still waiting,
Someone she had to go back to, to rise for
On every morning since. Something stirred me.

Because that mother's voice was all I wanted
To hear, the sound came through in another sense.
I cleared my throat and knew I had stayed too long.
The pan had done with spitting, and had sparked off
A torch's live plume. As I plunged my hands

In water soaking a towel, I wanted to know
What would happen to a flame when I had dressed it,
To know if something of its heat could be held
In a piece of cloth turning dry as a bone
Just as surely as my own sleeves would dry out.

The Cape of Good Hope

for my father-in-law

Always, in this climate, the sun threatens
To break through. To watch the outgoing tide
He walks to the bay window, a triptych

Of ocean, ocean, ocean, his whole life
A journey out from deep in the heartland
To the water's edge, an English coastline.

Although the silent mayday of his gaze
Does not stay the distance, a response comes
With the first gust of new weather in his bones.

An old memory takes flight, a childhood
Friend returns again. Their spirits are raised
In the guise of boys in the guise of men.

Inland, he asks the widower's question,
'What news of my angel?' His friend replies,
'We all settled, as we always said we would,

On that other shore which we call the Cape
Of Good Hope. Your wife is young, her age reduced
To the number of years that you loved her.

She looks forward to the same day as you do.
I'll tell you what you'll find when you get there.
Her photo in your wallet is your passport.

For all the associations that they hold
Your keepsakes will be honoured in full
As reminiscence is the legal tender,

Crystal-clear memories with no ill effects,
No medicine, no sipping at the spoonful,
And, if you so desire, we can give you

An immortal's capacity for drink.
But start with the celestial pool-table.
I'll call you when the time comes. You can break ...'

When he thinks he's alone, the widower wakes
And walks the whole length of his room, a journey
To the bay window, heavenly starlight

And ocean, ocean, ocean.

Sketch

In a café basement, off the kitchen
Sitting up in a light-well, is a wire sculpture
A slender woman, her steely fingers
Splayed, pushed against the glass as if she knows
Not me but everyone I could be.

So I should note the look on her face as tense
And wary as I am, curious to know
These hard lines and what to read between them.
She is a model's study of the artist
Though it isn't me she would catch exactly.

A waitress raises the pad in her palm
As if a still-life of apples in a bowl
Was there to render quickly in soft lead.
What if she could offer the cross-hatched fruit
To the overcast, breezed-through, chicken-wired

Figure whose blood-line would carry a fence-pulse?
The world upstairs is calling in the light.
Below the street she alone has caught the sun:
A brightening filament, an optimist
In the summer when her glass door is opened

And oven-heat escapes, her transparent hope
An after-image etched on air for as long
As we can draw breath, our anticipation
Pencilled in. The waitress who walks through the swing-door
Will not be the one who comes back.

The Mermaid

The part of him that was water
Poured itself out. Pooled with my own
His well-drawn stories keep afloat
Our *sometime soon*, another day
Out of the sun, falling headlong
Into the blue like the lost boy
Icarus, who, he said, had flown.

He was pearl-skinned, treading water
Wanting to ground flipperless feet
In a small-pond stance, far away
From the stingray's flourishing cape,
His tight lips sealing a bubble
A spirit-level resisting
Its flight, or the idea of flight.

Surfacing for cavernous air
He breathed a word in my ear
The secret in a shell's whisper
Safe as the age of my pebble-
Smooth skin. This barely marked touchstone
Holds light as distant memory
His hands on the small of my back

Swayed by the whale song's medium.
He was held by a single note
A softened cry that might have been
A parent calling over sleep.
I made out a bleary anchor
Stirring, lifting its heavy head
To be steadied, steadied and weighed,

Raised now like the boy lost sight of,
Me in his wake, still tantalised
As a drop of rain, for I saw
No fish in the sea worth his salt
On my tail, when I gave myself
Up, drawn to the end of the line
Like a fisherman's shameless catch

To the boat's eclipse of the sun.
I saw the stingray and wanted
The tongue's unspoken fluency
Feeling the moon rippling through me
Calm herself for the boy to read
His face and fathom the water's
Depth, reflections of hard coral

Still wavering, his sounding line
Drawing out everything I knew
Of him – the boy in the legend,
The Breughel, the poem, even,
Whose ship staying true to its course
Had slipped its moment. Through the hull
I heard his footfall and touched it

For the vibration.

Aeolian Harp Player

i

Since you read me that piece by the woman in Shanghai
On her seemingly genteel English companions
Who treated her to one of their adventures
Away from servants, in a tucked-away courtyard
To barter with a gatekeeper they shouldn't have known,
I think of that bare-walled room, and the old man's distance
From the grass mat and our own correspondent, on whom
He turned his back to see more clearly who she wasn't
And, from his shallow-bodied, long-necked lute, sent a note
On its maiden flight to find its mark, and not, like him,
Grow old on the journey.

He hasn't forgotten the hard-boiled egg,
Smooth as the razor-stroked skin his father
Let him touch. Every morning the bristly nest
Was lathered, but I have to remember
For him the nimble blade, the follow-through, the bird
That skims across a clearing in the wood

Its name flying beyond it. Deep in the wood
By a pool of yolk, a big boy has pricked the egg
He stole, while another has blown the bird
That would have pecked the shell my father
Might have known. The old man could climb, remember,
Watch an upturned face recede until the nest

Showed one jewel left in its thorny crown. A nest
Of mouthfuls, recycled leaves and deadwood
Is feeding a thought I remember
He spoke of, 'Something that grows like an egg,
Beyond itself', taking a mother and father
Beyond themselves. Not a speck of a bird

Migrating to nowhere, but the gift of a bird
Its song in the branches, sung from the nest
Long-abandoned and seasoned by one grey feather
In the one tree that matters in the wood.
Now the light is failing I ease the egg
From his palm and, for both of us, remember

My father, calling us home in the wood.
Though he can't quite place that bird in the nest,
Is the warm egg all he will remember?

Summoning the Seals

What brings the seals out at night peeping over the waves
Is the beached woman like one of their own delivered
By the tide, her pair of shades and a Baedeker
And a tube of lotion put to one side. Its cool balm
The length of her back is calling down the stars
As more seals under the water yield themselves up
So their pelts will be lightened as their dark eyes shine
Before the laid-out towel and a calm unwinded flame.

In my country you can sink your hands and a pulse
Makes waves, and every night each of us out before dawn
Takes a breath to call out her name with salt on the tongue.
Away from those sound-asleep and not a soul in sight
We are fishermen missing the fluency of bream
Or the face of the moon, distracted, turning to light.

ii

Just as new weather is forecast by mended bones
For years after the break, so her heart resembles
An aeolian harp, played by no one but the breeze
In the wake of a bird that has flown half-way around
The cup from her willow-pattern china, away from
Or towards the songbird's plum tree, small world tilted
On its axis, placed in the *trembleuse* of the saucer
As the newspaper she was reading collapses,
Pushing out air, a gasp from a landscape that can
No longer withhold an echo as she ventures out
To harvest the flat thrumming fields of the wind-farmer.

An aeolian harp has six strings of varying thickness, tuned to the same
note and played by the wind, making an 'unearthly' sound.

Forest of Memory

The tree falls again, just as I remember,
Through crackling branches, flushing out the bird.
Its flapping, clapping exit leaves the speckled egg
For me to hold, replace and watch over the nest
And the view below, a dog unleashed in the wood
Barking at the sound of my name, my father

Calling home his children, recalling his father
Rooted to the spot. He doesn't remember
His son in the branches, just walking through the wood,
Falling into line but following the bird
On its drunken weaving flight back to the nest,
To fingerprints fading from the unclaimed egg.